Kacey Musgraves

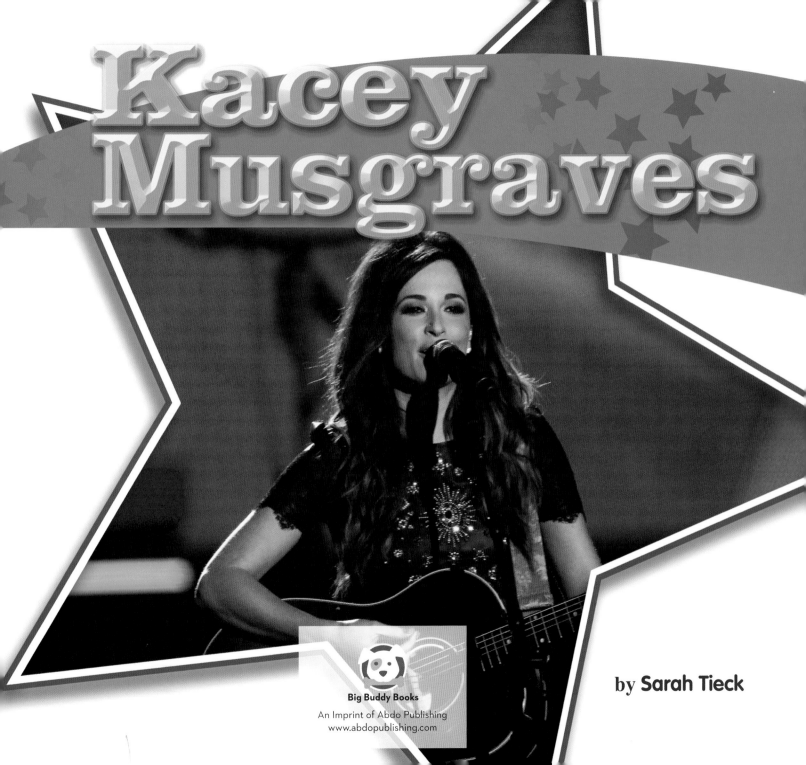

by **Sarah Tieck**

Big Buddy Books
An Imprint of Abdo Publishing
www.abdopublishing.com

www.abdopublishing.com

Published by Abdo Publishing, a division of ABDO, PO Box 398166, Minneapolis, Minnesota 55439.
Copyright © 2015 by Abdo Consulting Group, Inc. International copyrights reserved in all countries. No part
of this book may be reproduced in any form without written permission from the publisher. Big Buddy Books™
is a trademark and logo of Abdo Publishing.

Printed in the United States of America, North Mankato, Minnesota.
092014
012015

Cover Photo: Wade Payne/Invision/AP.
Interior Photos: ASSOCIATED PRESS (pp. 11, 15, 21); FilmMagic (p. 27); Getty Images (pp. 9, 13, 19, 23, 25); Getty
    Images for CMT (p. 29); Donn Jones/Invision/AP (p. 7); NBCU Photo Bank via Getty Images (p. 17); Al Powers/
    Powers Imagery/Invision/AP (p. 5); WireImage (p. 18).

Coordinating Series Editor: Rochelle Baltzer
Contributing Editors: Megan M. Gunderson, Marcia Zappa
Graphic Design: Maria Hosley

Library of Congress Cataloging-in-Publication Data

Tieck, Sarah, 1976-
  Kacey Musgraves : country music star / Sarah Tieck.
    pages cm. -- (Big buddy biographies)
  Audience: 7-11.
  ISBN 978-1-62403-571-5
1. Musgraves, Kacey--Juvenile literature. 2. Country musicians--United States--Biography--Juvenile literature. I.
Title.
  ML3930.M94T54 2015
  782.421642092--dc23
  [B]
                    2014026417

Kacey Musgraves

Contents

Kacey sings her own music.
She also writes for other stars.

Singing Star

Kacey Musgraves is a country singer and songwriter. She has won awards for her hit albums and songs. Kacey is also known for appearing on the television show *Nashville Star*.

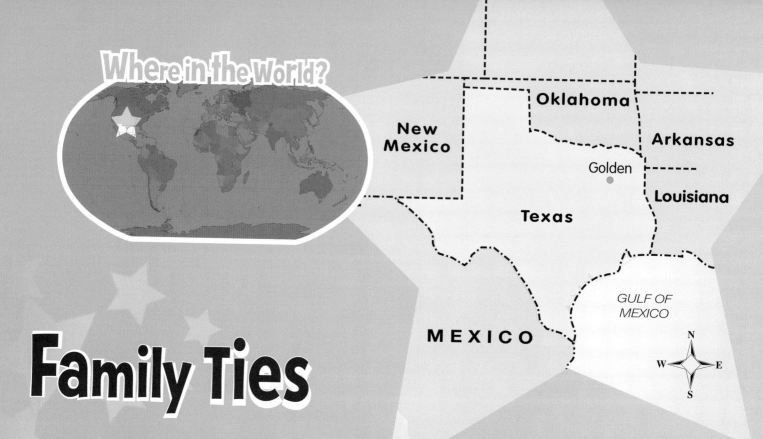

Family Ties

Kacey Lee Musgraves was born on August 21, 1988. Her parents are Karen and Craig Musgraves. Her younger sister is Kelly.

Kacey grew up in the small town of Golden, Texas. Her mother was an artist, and her parents owned a print shop. Kacey's family encouraged her to be creative and work hard to reach her dreams.

Kacey uses stories and experiences from her youth in Texas to write and perform songs.

Music Lover

As a young girl, Kacey discovered a love of music and began writing songs. Her first song was called "Notice Me." Around age eight, she started singing for audiences. Her first **performance** was in church.

Kacey built her skills singing in nearby towns. She performed onstage in **opry houses** with live bands. This helped her improve as a performer.

Kacey's first instrument was the mandolin. Today, she also plays guitar, banjo, and harmonica.

9

Kacey began learning to play the guitar around age 12. Her teacher, John DeFoore, had her write a song for each lesson. Then, he'd help her improve it. Kacey got comfortable trying out new ideas.

After high school, Kacey **released** her first album. It is called *Movin' On*. Soon after, she moved to Austin, Texas. She put out more albums in 2003 and 2007. They were called *Wanted: One Good Cowboy* and *Kacey Musgraves*.

DeFoore is a well-known music teacher. Kacey is one of many musicians who have learned from him.

Nashville Star

In 2007, Kacey took part in *Nashville Star*. This was a singing competition on television. Kacey came in seventh place. Being on the show made her think about moving to Nashville, Tennessee.

In 2008, Kacey did move to Nashville. She wanted to be a professional songwriter. Nashville is known as a center for country music.

Nashville Star helped Kacey (*top, second from left*) and other young singers get a start in country music.

Talented Singer

In Nashville, Kacey worked with many people to build her **career**. She wrote songs and sang **demos** for other singers. She worked on her own music, too.

In 2012, Kacey **released** a song called "Merry Go 'Round." In spring 2013, she released the album *Same Trailer Different Park*. It quickly became a hit!

When Kacey's album came out, critics especially noticed her strong songwriting skills.

KACEY
MUSGRAVES
SAME TRAILER DIFFERENT PARK

mercury

15

Same Trailer Different Park had many popular songs. "Merry Go 'Round" was one of them. Others included "Follow Your Arrow," "Blowin' Smoke," and "Keep It to Yourself."

In March 2013, Kacey performed live on *Today*.

Award Winner

In 2014, Kacey won two **Grammy Awards** for her music! She won Best Country Album for *Same Trailer Different Park*. And "Merry Go 'Round" won for Best Country Song.

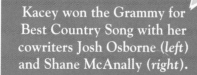

Kacey won the Grammy for Best Country Song with her cowriters Josh Osborne (*left*) and Shane McAnally (*right*).

Kacey sang "Follow Your Arrow" at the 2014 Grammys.

Songwriter

Kacey writes songs for herself and for other singers. In 2011, Miranda Lambert recorded "Mama's Broken Heart" for her album *Four the Record*. Kacey had helped write it.

Kacey cowrote the song "Undermine" with Trent Dabbs. Actors Hayden Panettiere and Charles Esten sang it on the television show *Nashville*.

Loretta Lynn (*above*), John Prine (*top*), and Patty Griffin (*right*) inspire Kacey's music. They are respected country music singers and songwriters.

A Singer's Life

Kacey works hard on her music. She helps write her songs. After much practice, she records them. Kacey spends a lot of time working on her albums in a **studio**.

Kacey enjoys singing live for her fans.

23

As she's worked to build her **career**, Kacey has gone on tour. She travels and **performs** live concerts. When Kacey is not writing, recording, or performing, she attends events and meets fans. Her fans are always excited to see her!

Sometimes, Kacey does radio interviews.

Off the Stage

Kacey spends free time with her family and friends. She likes to help others. In 2013, Kacey **performed** as part of Katy Perry's "We Can Survive" **charity** show. It raised money to help young women with breast cancer.

Sara Quin, Sara Bareilles, Katy Perry, Kacey, Ellie Goulding, Bonnie McKee, and Tegan Quin (*left to right*) all performed at the "We Can Survive" charity show.

Buzz

Kacey's work as a singer and songwriter continues to grow. In summer 2014, she toured with singer Katy Perry. Fans are excited for more music from Kacey Musgraves!

Kacey and Katy are friends offstage.

Snapshot

⭐**Name**: Kacey Lee Musgraves

⭐**Birthday**: August 21, 1988

⭐**Hometown**: Golden, Texas

⭐**Appearance**: *Nashville Star*

⭐**Albums**: *Movin' On, Wanted: One Good Cowboy, Kacey Musgraves, Same Trailer Different Park*

Important Words

career work a person does to earn money for living.

charity a group or a fund that helps people in need.

competition (kahm-puh-TIH-shuhn) a contest between two or more persons or groups.

demo a recording to show off a new song.

Grammy Award any of the awards given each year by the National Academy of Recording Arts and Sciences. Grammy Awards honor the year's best accomplishments in music.

opry house a performance hall featuring live country music. Usually multiple artists perform at each event.

perform to do something in front of an audience. A performance is the act of doing something, such as singing or acting, in front of an audience.

professional (pruh-FEHSH-nuhl) working for money rather than only for pleasure.

release to make available to the public.

studio a place where music is recorded.

Websites

To learn more about Big Buddy Biographies, visit **booklinks.abdopublishing.com**. These links are routinely monitored and updated to provide the most current information available.

Index